S0-BFC-902

MAKERSPACES

GETTING THE MOST OUT OF
MAKERSPACES
TO BUILD
ROBOTS

JACOB COHEN

ROSEN
PUBLISHING

New York

Published in 2015 by The Rosen Publishing Group, Inc.
29 East 21st Street, New York, NY 10010

Copyright © 2015 by The Rosen Publishing Group, Inc.

First Edition

Library of Congress Cataloging-in-Publication Data

Cohen, Jacob (Engineer)
Getting the most out of makerspaces to build robots/Jacob Cohen.
    pages cm.—(Makerspaces)
Audience: Grades 5–8.
Includes bibliographical references and index.
ISBN 978-1-4777-7819-7 (library bound)—ISBN 978-1-4777-7821-0 (pbk.)—ISBN 978-1-4777-7822-7 (6-pack)
1. Robotics—Juvenile literature. 2. Robots—Juvenile literature. I. Title.
TJ211.2.C64 2015
629.8'92—dc23

2014002174

Manufactured in the United States of America

CONTENTS

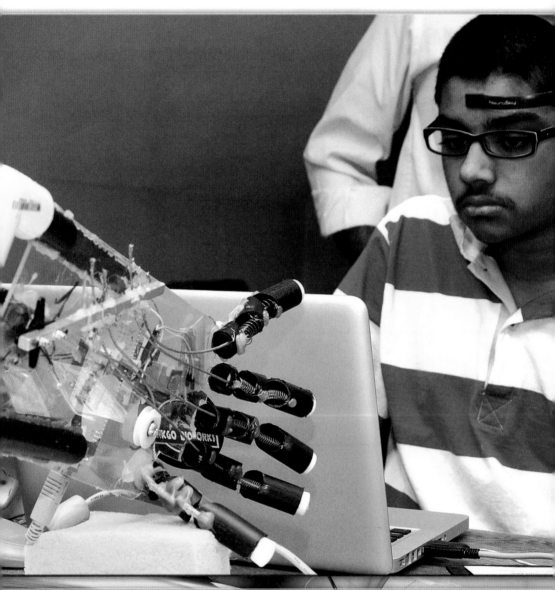

Fifteen-year-old Shiva Nathan moves his Arduino-powered robotic arm with his mind. His brainwaves are interpreted by a MindWave headset, where they are converted into movement commands.

Think about the world in which you live. How many robots do you interact with in your daily life? If you said none, think again. Robots are everywhere in today's world: cars with cruise control, dishwashers, and even smartphones. All of these can be considered robots because they automate tasks. Robots are a major part of our daily life, and this trend will continue to grow.

A new trend in the STEM (science, technology, engineering, and mathematics) field is the makerspace movement. A makerspace, as the name implies, is a local work space where people known as makers can come to work on their personal projects. Many of these projects are robots. Makerspaces feature shared resources such as tools, books, and other equipment. Creating a community space enables makers to pool their resources and knowledge to make bigger and better things.

Recently, makerspaces have begun springing up in public libraries. This movement brings two incredible resources into one location. Not only do makers working in these unique spaces receive the benefits of a standard makerspace, but they also have additional library resources just steps away. Libraries across the country have seen the power of STEM education, and they have stepped in to support it by embracing the makerspace movement.

A makerspace is the perfect place to build a robot. Most spaces feature the tools and expertise necessary to achieve success in your robot design. The tools available will make it easier to build your robot and troubleshoot any issues you may run into. More importantly, fellow makers are always there to help you with any challenge you may face along the way. Some makerspaces have robot builder groups or teams with scheduled meetings to work on their robots.

This resource is intended to guide you through the many varieties of robots you can build and to show you where to start. You will be introduced to robot concepts along with various hardware and software options available to you. Sometimes this will be dictated by what equipment is available to you at your local library, makerspace, or both, but many times you will determine what type of robot you want to build. With all of the amazing options out there, it will be difficult to narrow down your ideal robot platform.

Finally, you will be briefly introduced to some popular robotics competitions. It is at this point where you get to apply all of the knowledge you've gained working with your robots. Robots in these competitions come in many different sizes and require different team capabilities. Makerspaces are a great home for many of these teams, as you will have access there to the tools and knowledge required for success.

Remember, when you begin building your robot, it may be challenging. You may get stuck or frustrated, but there are always resources available to you to help you succeed. Working in your local makerspace means that there are fellow makers there to help you solve your problems and continue advancing your robot. Building robots can be incredibly challenging, yet it just might be the most rewarding project you'll ever work on.

CHAPTER ONE

WHAT EXACTLY IS A ROBOT?

Before you begin building your robot it is important to understand the robotics field and the various subsets of robots. *Merriam-Webster's* dictionary defines a robot as "a machine that can do the work of a person and that works automatically or is controlled by a computer." This is an intentionally broad definition that encompasses both automation and mechanization. Robots may run by themselves, autonomously, or be controlled, or teleoperated, by humans. They come in all shapes and sizes, from the size of a large SUV to a couple of nanometers. Robots are used everywhere: in manufacturing, education, entertainment, science…the list goes on and on.

TYPES OF ROBOTS

There are five main classifications of ground robots: turtles, rovers, humanoids, fixed/arms, and walkers. Other types of robots include aerial vehicles and underwater robots. This resource focuses on ground vehicles, but these concepts could be easily adapted to other types of robots.

TURTLES

Most early innovation in robotics was done using turtle robots: compact vehicles with two drive wheels and a third free-spinning or steering wheel. The first autonomous robots were developed in the late 1940s by an American-born British scientist, William Grey Walter, in an effort to demonstrate how the human brain operates. He referred to these machines as Machina speculatrix and named the first two Elmer and Elsie. Observers described the movement of these robots as similar to that of a tortoise, thus the name turtle robots.

An early version of William Grey Walter's analog turtle robot, this robot has sensors enabling it to detect light and touch.

ROVERS

Commonly used in space exploration, rovers have been traversing alien surfaces for years. These vehicles are designed to navigate difficult, unknown terrain. Rovers are routinely teleoperated, as they exist to perform scientific experiments. Scientists and engineers back on Earth communicate where they want the rover to move, and the robot autonomously navigates from point to point. The most famous and successful rovers are NASA's Mars rovers, beginning with Sojourner, launched in 1997, which operated for about three months. In 2003, NASA launched Spirit, which operated for nearly seven years, and Opportunity, which is still exploring Mars today. NASA launched Curiosity in 2011, and it has surpassed its two-year expected life span.

HUMANOIDS

When most people picture a robot, they picture a humanoid. Used mainly for research, these robots are designed to resemble a human body. They can be designed to work with human tools, to play a sport, or even to be a companion. Japan is the chief pioneer in humanoid robotics. The most famous humanoid is Honda's ASIMO, which has become a robotic spokesperson for STEM education. Another popular humanoid is the NASA/GM Robonaut, designed to operate on the International Space Station and assist astronauts by leveraging its extreme dexterity.

Fixed/Arms

Believe it or not, robotic arms are some of the most commonly used robots in industry. They are used in manufacturing to perform complex but repetitive tasks autonomously. A key characteristic of these arms is the end effector, the actuator or device attached to the arm used to perform a specific task. An example of an end effector is a motor used to rotate a screw or a welder that melds two pieces of metal. Many times an arm can be combined with another type of robot, such as a turtle or rover, to create a more complicated robot capable of executing a repeatable task on the move. All of NASA's Mars rovers feature numerous arms used for experimentation.

Honda's ASIMO demonstrates its dexterity by holding a tray of coffee. This humanoid robot has two arms integrated into its overall design.

WALKERS

As opposed to rovers, walker robots feature legs instead of wheels as the basis for movement. They are significantly more advanced than wheeled robots because of their complex motion. These robots are modeled after insects and other animals in an effort to achieve successful all-terrain navigation. A popular example of a walker robot is Boston Dynamics' BigDog, which boasts four legs, the ability to navigate across ice, and the ability to recover from being knocked over. This technology is of major interest to the military, which could use these robots as mules to carry heavy loads through rough terrain.

BigDog robots, being controlled by a portable control unit, show their ability to carry heavy loads while walking around a military base.

ROBOT ARCHITECTURE

When designing a robot, it is important to take into consideration all major physical aspects. Mobile robots have five major subsystems: chassis, power supply, control system, motors/effectors, and sensors. All of these subsystems are vital for robot operation.

DARPA CHALLENGES

DARPA, the advanced research arm of the U.S. Department of Defense, occasionally hosts robotics challenges that bring out the best in the industry. It began hosting the Grand Challenge, where robots had to autonomously traverse 150 miles (241.4 kilometers) across the Mojave Desert. In 2007, DARPA hosted the more difficult Urban Challenge, where robots had to navigate a makeshift city complete with homes, streets, cars, speed limits, and pedestrians. Robots were provided with a map of the area and start and end points. They were required to navigate between these points in less than six hours while avoiding accidents and obeying traffic regulations. Multiple robots navigated the course at the same time. The winner of the competition was Tartan Racing, of Carnegie Mellon University, with a time just longer than four hours. The DARPA Urban Challenge initiated the current development of autonomous vehicles that automakers have focused on recently.

CHASSIS

The chassis is the base structure of the robot. All components are attached to the chassis. It is extremely important to get this part of the robot right, as design flaws can ripple throughout the rest of the robot. Common chassis materials include metals, usually aluminum; plastics; and composites, such as carbon fiber. Recently, 3-D-printed chassis have become popular in smaller robots. Most makerspaces have access to a 3-D printer, allowing you to have a hand in designing the core of your robot.

POWER SUPPLY

Robots are electronic devices, meaning they require power. Rechargeable lithium-ion batteries or standard alkaline batteries power most mobile robots. However, there are robots that are powered by solar panels or other, less common batteries. In most cases, the instructions included with a robot kit or microcontroller will describe which type of battery is required.

CONTROL SYSTEM

All logic operations take place in the control system. Most robots use a microcontroller, though the most basic robots get by with analog components to perform logic operations. Robots that use a microcontroller require software to describe the robot behavior. Control systems and programming are a major focus of later chapters.

An open-sourced Netduino, powered by a 32-bit ARM microcontroller, is shown with a clear breadboard and prototype boards used for testing electronic circuit designs.

MOTORS/EFFECTORS

This subsystem is responsible for all of the robot's movements. Common components included are direct current (DC) and brushless motors, servos, and actuators.

SENSORS

Autonomous robots rely exclusively on sensors, as they are the only inputs to the control system. They serve as the basis for every decision made in the control system. Common sensors include switches (touch), photocells (light), ultrasound sensors (distance), microphones (sound), and GPS sensors (position).

CHAPTER TWO

USING MAKERSPACES TO BUILD ANALOG ROBOTS

If you want to focus on the hardware aspect of robots, if programming isn't your thing, or if you just love electronics, analog robots are where you should start. Analog robots use electronic circuitry to achieve simple goals. These goals include something as simple as moving forward, moving toward or away from a light source, and even being remotely controlled via a wired controller. The first turtle robots, Elmer and Elsie, were analog, operating with vacuum tubes and a photocell to find a light source. Other common analog robots include underwater remotely operated vehicles (ROVs), where the vehicle is submerged underwater with a wire leading to a remote control on land.

CIRCUIT-BASED ANALOG ROBOTS

Building a circuit-based robot from scratch

Printed circuit boards (PCBs), such as this robust one from a radio server, are everywhere. Look around and you'll find plenty of them in your daily life.

is a difficult task to attempt on your own. Fortunately, there are numerous kits out there where the design work has been done for you. These kits are great for roboticist rookies in that they provide an introduction to soldering and electronics without the complexities of circuit design. A good kit will come with a printed circuit board (PCB) with holes to solder on electronic components included in the kit.

A great example of a circuit-based analog robot is the light-following Herbie robot. The kit for Herbie includes all the necessary electronics and the PCB to build a fully functioning analog robot. Even better, with a bit of research you can find the schematic for Herbie and build it yourself on a breadboard or prototype circuit board. Herbie uses an operational amplifier (op-amp)

BEAM ROBOTICS

Most modern analog robots are a type of biology, electronics, aesthetics, and mechanics (BEAM) robot. This subset of robotics was pioneered by Dr. Mark Tilden of WowWee RoboSapien fame. By using only analog components, these robots are able to make decisions in a similar fashion to biological neurons. These robots operate via a behavior-based control system developed at the Massachusetts Institute of Technology (MIT) by Dr. Rodney Brooks. This control strategy enables advanced behavior to emerge from a collection of simple logical operations. BEAM robots employ this strategy to add capabilities such as obstacle detection.

in a differential configuration to determine which light sensor sees the brighter light. This is how it chooses which direction to turn in and which motor should move.

Makerspaces are the perfect place to work on a robot like this, as you are almost guaranteed to find someone there who is an electronics and soldering expert. A good makerspace will have soldering stations featuring soldering irons and other equipment to make robot assembly a breeze.

UNDERWATER ROVS

If nautical robots are more your style, take a look at underwater ROVs. Building one of these will provide an

A Sea Perch ROV, controlled from outside of the pool it is in, scores a ring in an underwater bucket as part of a game.

introduction to the concepts of waterproofing and the dynamics of underwater motion. Kits are available online and come complete with all parts and instructions for building an operational underwater ROV. For those with more experience, MIT has developed the Sea Perch kit for educational purposes. The Sea Perch construction manual contains all information necessary to build a vehicle, including the parts list. If you choose to build one of these, you will need to acquire all parts on your own. However, you may find some of the parts, like PVC pipes, used for the chassis, available in a makerspace.

This section covered the only type of robot that will work without programming. The next chapter will cover programming, which is essential for advanced robot operation.

CHAPTER THREE

MAKE YOUR ROBOT A GENIUS: PROGRAMMING LANGUAGES

Complex robots are worthless without software. You can build the most complicated robot in the world, but if you can't control it, what good is it? This is where software comes in, and that is why you should be aware of the programming languages available to you. This section will cover the standard programming languages used throughout the field along with languages specific to certain microcontrollers.

INDUSTRY STANDARD LANGUAGES

Although most microcontrollers used in educational robots do not use these languages, it is important to have an understanding of what is out there. Microcontrollers you will be using will typically use simplified versions of these languages.

Computers speak in ones and zeros, or binary code. Eventually all code will be converted from text that you can understand into binary, which the computer can interpret.

C

Developed in the early 1970s, C is the most common programming language used today. It is used in everything from microcontrollers to computers because it allows programmers extensive control of system resources. This is good and bad because programmers can end up in potentially hazardous situations causing unexpected errors. C is the language of choice when dealing with limited on-chip memory.

C++

Although it sounds similar, C++ is effectively an extension of C. This language takes C and adds the concept of objects, making C++ an object-oriented programming (OOP) language. OOP is a complicated concept, but the basic idea is that objects feature data fields and methods specific to themselves. The goal is to create modular code that can be reused efficiently. OOP is a difficult concept to master, but it is vital for the modern programmer to understand.

JAVA

Of the industry standard languages, Java is the easiest to start with because it provides safety features that protect the programmer from doing things he or she should avoid. Java abstracts many of the low-level programming concepts away from the programmer and manages them itself while providing full OOP functionality. If you're looking to start programming without a robot, Java is the language to start with.

LABVIEW

The visual programming language LabVIEW was developed by National Instruments (NI) for use in automation systems and scientific experimentation. Recently, it has made its way into the world of robots, as it can be easier for people without programming experience.

ROBOT PROGRAMMING LANGUAGES

Different from standard programming languages, robot programming languages are designed to work with specific microcontrollers and kits. Easy-to-follow tutorials are available online for all of these languages, including specific instructions on building and programming different types of robots.

Lego NXT-G and EV3

These languages are used for the Lego Mindstorms bricks and are powered by NI's LabVIEW. This software is graphics based, meaning the programmer can drag and drop blocks to create a program for the brick. NXT-G (next generation) is the older, but still common, software for Lego's NXT microcontroller. EV3 (third evolution) is compatible with the NXT and used for Lego's newer EV3 microcontroller. These languages are perfect for introduction to programming concepts and to get a Lego robot up and running quickly.

Arduino

The Arduino integrated development environment (IDE) was developed to be cross-platform, meaning you can program an Arduino on any operating system. The language itself is designed to look similar to C but with simplified syntax. With that said, the Arduino software does not prevent the programmer from accessing the complex features of the microcontroller, but it does not require the programmer to work with them.

RobotC

RobotC is a simplified version of C designed by Carnegie Mellon University for use with common microcontrollers, including Lego's NXT and EV3, the VEX Cortex and PIC, and the Arduino microcontrollers. RobotC is a good compromise between simple and complex programming languages that allows both novice and experienced programmers to feel comfortable developing in the environment. As the name implies, RobotC is the best language to work with when programming an educational robot.

LEARNING TO PROGRAM

Getting started in programming can be a major challenge, but every programmer has done it. Fortunately, resources to learn how to program have greatly improved, and they are only getting better. Local libraries and makerspaces will have books available that will help guide you through any programming language available. For those who prefer something more interactive, there are countless websites devoted to teaching coding. Many sites are designed to teach general coding practice, like www.code.org and www.codeacademy.com. Once you've mastered your programming best practices, you can move on to learning individual languages. The creators of most languages have provided tutorials, though there are usually other tutorial sites out there that may be more beneficial. The languages used on the programming platforms described in this resource all feature extensive documentation and curricula to help you master them. Make use of these. Going through the curriculum first will save you hours of troubleshooting later.

GETTING ASSISTANCE

Programming can be challenging to learn. There are resources available to help you. If you're working in a makerspace, ask around. Everyone is there to learn, and they are usually happy to help. There are countless resources available online. Search

around for the problem you're having; usually the solution will already be out there. If it's not, there are programming websites, such as www .stackoverflow.com, with users who love answering questions. The most important thing is not to get discouraged; programming is fun and arguably the most important part of robotics.

Lego NXT-based robots, programmed with NXT-G, navigate an FLL table *(top)* and an obstacle course *(bottom)*.

CHAPTER FOUR

LEGO MINDSTORMS: MORE THAN A BUCKET OF BLOCKS

There is something magical about Lego Mindstorms kits. Everyone, from kindergarteners to college students to professional engineers, is challenged and entertained by them. They are used in elementary schools to teach programming basics and in middle schools to teach automation. They are used in high schools to teach robotics, in colleges for introduction to engineering, and in industry for research. Hobbyists have used the NXT to build automated paper-airplane-folding machines and Rubik's Cube–solving robots (the CubeStormer). The potential of these platforms is limitless.

The first Lego Mindstorms intelligent brick debuted in 1998 and was dubbed the Robotic Command eXplorer, or RCX. It was originally developed by MIT as a low-cost

This Lego Mindstorms robot can see where to navigate, not because of its eyes, but because of the color sensors attached to the front of the robot.

educational tool. Ever since, Lego has continued the development of these bricks with the NXT, followed by the EV3.

All of these robot kits feature the key components of a robot. The control system is the microcontroller brick. The chassis is provided by the Lego pieces. The power system is either standard alkaline batteries or an included lithium-ion battery pack. The motors/effectors are included in the form of Lego motors with built-in encoder sensors used to count rotations. Finally, every kit includes an assortment of sensors that interface directly with the bricks.

CHOOSING A SYSTEM

The NXT and EV3 are both fantastic systems, but there are differences between the two. The NXT is older and less powerful than the EV3 but has more documentation and tutorials available. It is powerful enough to support most robotics projects. The EV3 has an additional motor port as well as support for more sensors. Finally, the NXT kit is less expensive than the EV3 kit.

CHOOSING A PROGRAMMING LANGUAGE

Once you've decided on a system, you need to choose a programming language. The available languages are NXT-G/EV3 visual programming or RobotC text-based programming. For advanced projects RobotC is the better choice, as it gives the programmer more control. Other projects can use either language; it depends on your preference.

GETTING IT RUNNING

After deciding on a language, you need to install the proper firmware on the brick. Each development environment will have a way to install or update to the proper firmware version. A quick firmware reflash will usually fix any issues you run into with your brick.

LEGO MINDSTORMS COMMUNITY

Lego is a great advocate for innovation with its Mindstorms platform. It has set up an online community for builders to share their creations. This website is a great place to look for inspiration and ideas for your next project. Some projects are incredibly complicated, whereas others are significantly easier to build. When you're ready to move past the kit robots with included instructions, this site is a great place to start. Browse around and find a robot that's of interest to you.

At this point, you're ready to see something move. It is usually best to start by moving a motor or displaying a sensor input to the screen. This lets you slowly test each part before integrating them to build a robot. Once you've got the hang of it, you're ready to move on to designing and building your robot.

DESIGNING AND BUILDING THE ROBOT

Once you know how to make the robot move, you're able to begin designing your robot. If you've never built a Lego robot before, you're going to want to start with one of the robots included in the kit. All Mindstorms kits come with instructions to build multiple robot variations. If Lego's robots just don't seem cool enough for you, there are countless examples available in books and online. Starting by building a predesigned robot is important because it will provide you with a strong understanding of the parts and pieces before you design your own robot.

After you've built a Lego robot or two, you can move on to designing your own. When you first start off designing, a lot of work will be done by trial and error. This is a great way to learn because you will get to see your designs in action early on in the design process. As you gain more experience, you will be able to design more of your robot before ever picking up a Lego piece.

CONTROLLING YOUR ROBOT

Now that you've built your robot, it's time to get it running. The easiest way to test your robot is to run it in teleoperated mode. Mindstorms can be controlled via smartphone with an app available from Lego. The NXT is limited to Android, and the EV3 can be controlled with both iOS and Android smartphone operating systems. In case you're looking for more control, most development environments provide an option for controlling the robot with USB gaming controllers. These can be a challenge, but there is plenty of support out there. Teleoperated mode is a great way to show off what your robot can do, but the most advanced robots are always autonomous.

Getting your robot to move autonomously is easier than controlling a robot via remote control. It's getting it to move how you want it to that can be the tricky part. Moving a robot forward is a simple command. True autonomous routines take input from sensors to make decisions as the program runs. Take

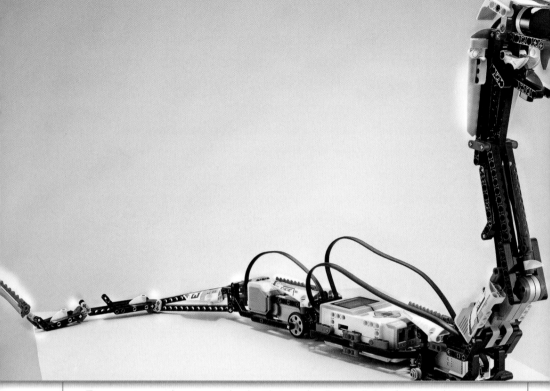

Reptar is a robotic snake built on the Lego Mindstorms' EV3 platform. It has the ability to communicate with iPhones, iPads, and iPod Touches using a Bluetooth wireless connection.

for example a simple line-following robot. This robot will have one or more light sensors attached that will detect the line. This will become simple Boolean (true or false) logic. Is the robot on the line? If yes, turn left. If no, turn right. This simple logic will keep a line-following robot on the left edge of a line.

Lego Mindstorms robots all come with tremendous sensor options. As a result, you can build an incredibly sophisticated robot using only Lego parts. Look around the Internet for videos of some of the autonomous Mindstorms robots to see just how powerful they can be. A local makerspace might just have some of these robots on display.

CHAPTER FIVE

MAKING WITH TETRIX AND MATRIX

Lego robots are cool, there's no question about it, but what if we could take a Mindstorms robot and make it bigger and stronger? That's where Tetrix and Matrix come in. These robot-building systems are all aluminum and are designed to be fully Lego Mindstorms compatible. This means that the powerful intelligent Lego bricks can be applied to larger, more powerful robots.

The benefit of both of these robot-building systems is that, like Legos, the parts are designed to fit together. This eliminates the need for power tools and other safety hazards in the build process. Metal support bars have predrilled hole patterns that match up with other accessory parts and enable the pieces to fit together at different angles. Gears all share the same tooth pattern and come in multiple sizes, allowing for many different gear ratios while keeping the overall parts list to a minimum.

Seventh- and eighth-graders begin assembling their Tetrix robot for their introduction to aviation and engineering class.

With stronger construction materials comes the need for stronger motors. Both systems include powerful DC motors and servos, along with the controllers designed to interface them with the Lego Mindstorms bricks.

Tetrix was originally developed as an educational platform for students to gain more experience in the mechanical engineering aspect of robot design. Soon after its release, Tetrix became the building material of the FIRST Tech Challenge (FTC) robotics competition. As a result of Tetrix's success, a competitor was formed, Matrix. This company offers a more affordable alternative to the Tetrix parts. For example, the gears are polycarbonate in-

WHAT TO DO WITH TETRIX?

There is no limit to what can be done with Tetrix metal paired with a Lego Mindstorms control system. A robot was designed for the FTC game Hot Shot! The robot was designed to capture, hold, and shoot Wiffle balls throughout the game. This particular robot featured an open center allowing it to hold more than forty-five of the sixty balls available on the field. The dual-shooter design was implemented using Tetrix wheels to fire at a higher rate than the competition. It was the only one of its kind built that year. Note the Lego sensors attached to the robot, including the compass sensor, IR sensor, and ultrasonic sensor. These sensors were used in the autonomous portion of the competition to help the robot navigate and score in the thirty-second autonomous period. This robot was built using Lego, Tetrix, aluminum sheet, and polycarbonate sheet. It was a finalist at the 2010 FIRST World Championship.

Tetrix robots, controlled with a Lego Mindstorms NXT, competing in the FIRST Tech Challenge (FTC), shoot Wiffle balls into high and low goals.

stead of aluminum. For most projects, this should not be an issue, making Matrix a valid alternative. Both Matrix and Tetrix parts are allowed in FTC robotics.

SAFETY

As you move to more advanced robots, safety becomes key. There are more aspects of the build process that require safety procedures, including the mechanical hardware, the electronics, and even the software. These robot platforms are perfectly safe as long as you follow proper safety procedure. Here are the basic safety rules according to Tetrix:

- To avoid possible injury, keep your fingers clear of metal gears and other pinch points while they are moving.
- Never pick up the robot when it is moving.
- Be sure power is off when the robot is not in operation.
- Do not operate the robot in wet environments.

There are many more safety procedures to keep in mind. An in-depth outline is available on the Tetrix website.

BUILDING AN ALUMINUM ROBOT

Although these parts are designed to fit together, they don't work together quite as well as Lego pieces. When building a structure, you will want to ensure that the pieces are square. This means that all angles are even before you tighten the fasteners. The quick and easy way to do this is to first connect all your pieces, but without tightening the screws all the way. Tighten them just enough so that the pieces are snug. At this point, adjust your frame so that all the parts are square. This is best done using alignment tools, but it can be done by eye if necessary. Once you're happy with the adjustments, you can tighten down the screws permanently. This is a simple build principle that will keep your robots sturdy for years to come.

Both build systems provide additional building tips, tricks, and instructions on their websites. These can be as simple as how to build a frame or as complex as how to build a fully functional robot. It's up to you where you want to start and how advanced you want to get. Beyond this there are countless additional resources available to you to advance your mechanical skills. A local makerspace will have tools to assist in the build process, as well as books and guides to help you through your assembly process.

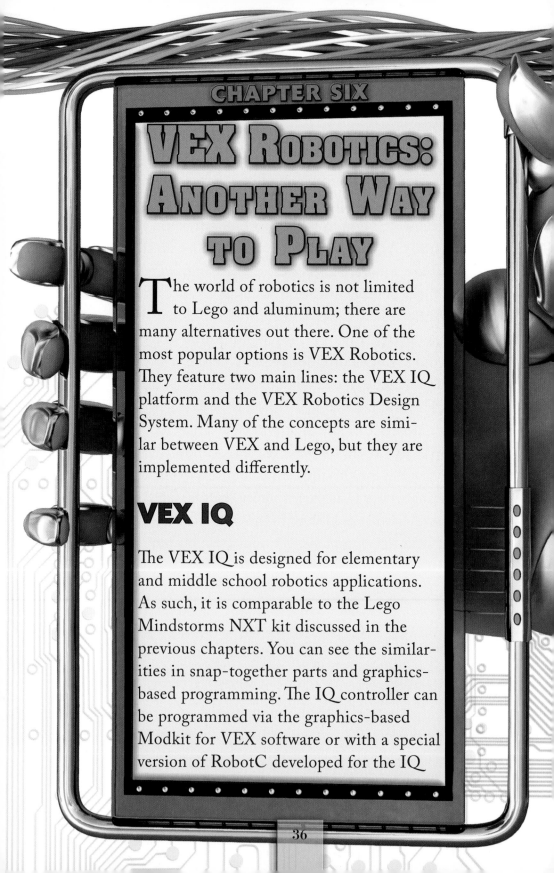

CHAPTER SIX

VEX Robotics: Another Way to Play

The world of robotics is not limited to Lego and aluminum; there are many alternatives out there. One of the most popular options is VEX Robotics. They feature two main lines: the VEX IQ platform and the VEX Robotics Design System. Many of the concepts are similar between VEX and Lego, but they are implemented differently.

VEX IQ

The VEX IQ is designed for elementary and middle school robotics applications. As such, it is comparable to the Lego Mindstorms NXT kit discussed in the previous chapters. You can see the similarities in snap-together parts and graphics-based programming. The IQ controller can be programmed via the graphics-based Modkit for VEX software or with a special version of RobotC developed for the IQ

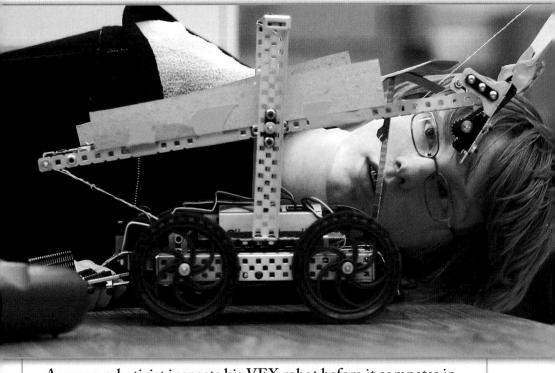

A young roboticist inspects his VEX robot before it competes in the VEX Robotics Challenge.

system. It also comes with preloaded programs to help get your robot up and running in no time.

A major advantage of the IQ system over the NXT is its twelve smart ports. These ports can handle any of the IQ accessories in any of the ports with no restrictions on device type. For example, if you wanted to run twelve motors, you could. By contrast, the NXT is limited to three motors and four sensors.

Because the VEX IQ system was designed with education in mind, VEX has provided curriculum free of charge online. Although some of it may be designed specifically for classroom use, it is still a great resource to get started with the system.

The VEX IQ system is the current underdog compared to the Mindstorms platform, but that does not mean that it's not a good option. The choice between the two will be specific to your project and preferences. Keep in mind there are other systems out there as well.

BUILDING A SQUAREBOT

When first getting started with the VEX system, you should always start by building a squarebot. This is effectively the beginner's program of VEX robots. Although this is a simple robot, it is a great way to become familiar with the properties of the metal and fasteners. You'll gain a feel for how the predrilled holes work together and how the gearing and axels intermesh. Once the squarebot is built, you will have to get it running. No matter what the physical robot looks like, getting the drive train running takes the same amount of effort. If you are more interested in the programming and sensor aspect of the robot, a squarebot is all the foundation you need to be able to build a robot with advanced logic. Simply mount your sensors on the chassis and begin developing your software. A squarebot can also serve as the foundation for a complicated manipulator, as it provides a solid base for advancement.

VEX ROBOTICS DESIGN SYSTEM

This is the original VEX system, and it has only improved since it was released. In general, people refer to this kit as VEX for short. The VEX robot-building system has been on the market since long before Tetrix showed up. These kits are the reason predrilled holes and metal designed to work together caught on. Unlike the Tetrix system, VEX is available in both steel and aluminum. Steel is cheaper and heavier and does not age as well compared to aluminum. If you have a weight limit, or you intend to display your robot for years, aluminum is the right choice. Otherwise, steel is the wallet-friendly option.

The ARM-based VEX Cortex Microcontroller features internal wireless "VEXnet" technology along with analog and digital I/O ports used for effector control and sensor input.

The VEX system features two microcontroller choices. The first is the original PIC microcontroller. This is the more affordable version, but it is rapidly becoming outdated. The second is the VEX Cortex Microcontroller, which features a much more powerful ARM-based processor. This controller will surely last into the future.

Both available microcontrollers feature eight motor ports and more than twenty input output (I/O) ports, used for sensor integration. Most important, both can be controlled with a wireless remote control.

The programming languages available for these controllers are easyC and RobotC. VEX created easyC as a graphics-based programming language, but it has evolved to support graphics for beginners and text-based programming for more experienced developers. As for RobotC, this is the most common text-based software used in this type of robot.

Overall, the VEX systems have great potential for any robot you want to build. It is up to you to compare all options and choose what system is best for you. Roboticists are great people to talk to for advice on which platform to choose for your project. Check out a makerspace near you and see if it has examples of these platforms. Many makerspaces will, and you may have the opportunity to work with their equipment.

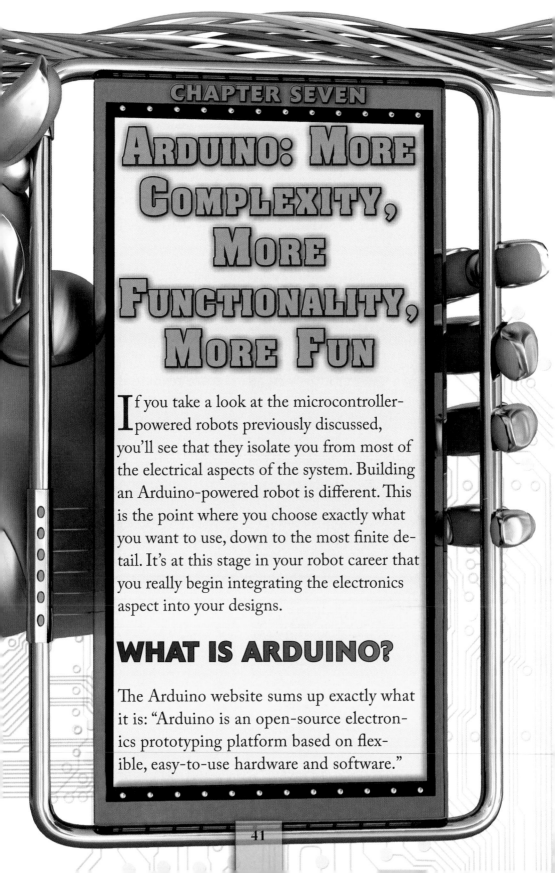

CHAPTER SEVEN

ARDUINO: MORE COMPLEXITY, MORE FUNCTIONALITY, MORE FUN

If you take a look at the microcontroller-powered robots previously discussed, you'll see that they isolate you from most of the electrical aspects of the system. Building an Arduino-powered robot is different. This is the point where you choose exactly what you want to use, down to the most finite detail. It's at this stage in your robot career that you really begin integrating the electronics aspect into your designs.

WHAT IS ARDUINO?

The Arduino website sums up exactly what it is: "Arduino is an open-source electronics prototyping platform based on flexible, easy-to-use hardware and software."

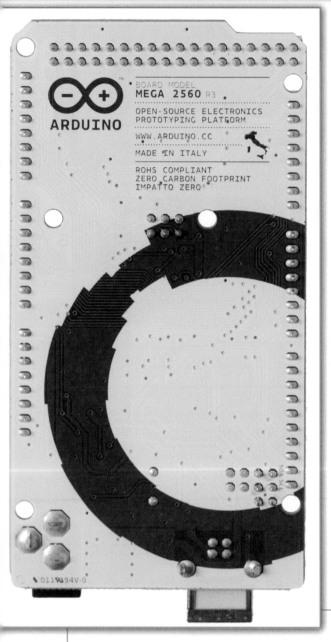

Although most people refer to Arduino as the board itself, Arduino is more than that: it is the full platform, including the board, development environment, software, and community.

Some credit Arduino for starting the maker-space revolution. Arduino is an affordable and relatively easy-to-use single-board microcontroller. The open-source community, which is a large part of the maker community, has been the key to Arduino's success. Today, the Arduino product line has expanded to include many different boards designed for different applications, including a

The Arduino Mega board is designed to be used anywhere by anyone. Roboticists, engineers, artists, and designers all have uses for an Arduino.

complete robot. A basic Arduino board with microcontroller and peripherals on the board can be had for around $20.

ARDUINO SOFTWARE

The Arduino IDE was developed in the Java programming language to be platform independent, meaning it runs on Windows, Mac, and Linux operating systems. The Arduino language itself is extremely similar to C, with a few small modifications to make development easier. An Arduino program is referred to as a sketch. Each sketch requires two functions: set up and loop. The set up function will run once when the board is first powered on or reset, followed by the loop function, which will run in an infinite, never-ending loop until the board is powered off.

Choosing Arduino means that you will have access to hundreds of resources in books and on websites featuring sample sketches with solutions to many of the design problems you will encounter. There will be code libraries available for almost anything you can think of, including controlling servos and motors, connecting to the Internet, reading sensors, controlling displays, and managing external memory, along with many others.

ARDUINO SHIELDS

Having the ability to interface with your own electronics is great, but sometimes it's easier to work with a device that has already been designed for you. Shields are electronics boards designed to be attached directly to the top of the Arduino board. Some shields are designed to be stacked, allowing you to add multiple features to one Arduino board.

A motor controller shield can be stacked on an Arduino controller for an easy interface with DC motors for a stronger, more robust robot.

Shields are available from many hobby retailers, both in store and online. Some of the more popular retailers are Adafruit Industries, SparkFun, and Amazon. The Arduino boards are able to control servos without the addition of a shield, but if you plan to have motors on your robot, you will need an external motor controller. Devices known as H-bridges are the most basic motor controllers. You could purchase these in an integrated circuit (IC) and wire the controller yourself, or you could purchase a shield with all of the electronics work done for you.

There are many other shields available with extensive capabilities beyond just robots. Shields exist to support a GPS sensor, a data logger, an LCD screen, Wi-Fi communication, and many other specific-use hardware options.

BUILDING YOUR ARDUINO ROBOT

If you've chosen Arduino as your control system, you are going to have to decide on the rest of your hardware, including your

BEATTY ROBOTICS

Located in North Carolina, Beatty Robotics, run by a father and his two daughters, is developing some of the most advanced Arduino robots ever built. They have built robots for museums, designed parts for manufacturers, and built both ground and aerial vehicles. The Mars rover model designed for the New York Hall of Science is equipped with many of the same types of sensors that are featured on the real rovers, including a thermal array sensor and sonar sensors. An Arduino Mega microcontroller paired with an Xbee radio for wireless control provides the processing power for the robot. This is a great example of the power available on Arduino Mega. Check out some other Beatty Robotics projects on their blog: www.beatty-robotics.com.

chassis, power supply, actuators, and sensors. First-time robot builders should find a predesigned kit that will include instructions on how to assemble and wire the complete robot hardware. These kits typically include everything you need to build a fully functional, autonomous robot. A good kit will have parts such as the chassis, motors, wheels, wires, power supply (either a rechargeable battery or an alkaline battery holder), breadboard, servo, and an ultrasonic distance sensor (or a similar sensor). Some kits will include the Arduino and shield as well, so keep that in mind when pricing kits. Arduino-powered robot kits range from $40 for a basic chassis to more than $1,000 for a larger robot with all the bells and whistles.

WHAT CAN I DO WITH MY ARDUINO ROBOT?

Undergraduate robotics classes build Arduino-powered robots. Throughout their semester, college students implement a new robot feature, such as light tracking or wall following, each week. These weekly projects culminate in a semester project that consists of a complex design such as a GPS navigating robot that would travel between waypoints (GPS locations) while detecting and avoiding obstacles along the way. These tasks may seem complicated, but they are achievable for anyone comfortable with Arduino. Instead of finishing your project in a week, you may take a month or more. But as long as you keep working on it, you'll get it working.

This track-based, line-follower robot is powered by an Arduino partnered with a motor controller shield and features two SparkFun IR sensors for line detection.

Working on your robot at your local makerspace may make your life easier. Anytime you get stuck, you can ask a fellow maker for help. If you're still stuck, check out an Arduino guidebook or look online for a reference. Keep in mind the maker community is there to help everywhere— in a makerspace or online.

CHAPTER EIGHT

COMPETITIONS: WHERE THE REAL FUN BEGINS

After honing your robot-building skills, you're going to want to apply them to new challenges. Competitions are the best, most fun way to do that. A robotics competition can work in many different ways. Sometimes robots will have to complete predefined tasks in a certain amount of time; other times robots will compete against other robots to see which can score the most points. Most competitions take place annually: the organization releases a game, teams get time to build their robots, and then teams attend the competition. No matter the competition format, you will find yourself challenged.

One thing most modern-day competitions have in common is that they are cooperative. This means that teams work together for greater success. Unless you're entering the BattleBots competition, the goal is not to break other robots. Instead, the goal is for all teams to compete at their best so that the best robot, or team, wins.

MAKERSPACE COMPETITIONS

Sometimes you want to start a little friendly competition among your fellow makers. This is the perfect time to set

Much like BattleBots and Robot Wars, these robots battle it out at the Combots Cup.

up a competition in-house. Find an old game from one of the competitions described below or brainstorm together to design your own. This is a great way to bring a makerspace together and work toward a common goal. If your local makerspace does not have enough people to host its own competition, or if you want to branch out into something new, it might be time to look into forming a team for an existing competition. Teams for these competitions can come from anywhere: makerspaces, families, youth organizations, schools, and more.

VEX ROBOTICS COMPETITIONS

You've been introduced to the VEX Robotics systems in an earlier chapter. In 2007, owing to the success of its products, VEX developed a series of competitions to continue challenging interested roboticists.

VEX IQ CHALLENGE

Designed for elementary and middle school students, ages eight to fourteen, the VEX IQ Challenge provides a playground for the IQ system. According to the VEX website, "VEX IQ Challenge teams will work together scoring points in Teamwork Matches, and also display their robot's skills individually in driver controlled and autonomous Skills Challenges." If you are in the age range and enjoy the IQ control system, this is the competition for you.

VEX Robotics Competition

For older, more experienced students, VEX created the VEX Robotics Competition (designed for middle and high school students, ages eleven to eighteen). In this competition, VEX asks students to build "robots designed to score the most points possible in qualification matches, elimination matches and Skills Challenges." This is the oldest, most successful VEX program.

VEX U

Unlike other robotics organizations, VEX has created a competition for college-aged (eighteen and older) students. In this competition, known as VEX U, students build a design for the same game used in the VEX Robotics Competition but with a few added parameters. The major difference is that teams are required to build two different-sized robots that must work together throughout the matches and challenges. VEX U is a great way for students who participated in VEX competitions in grade school to continue their robotics career through college.

FIRST ROBOTICS

The premier organization for furthering STEM education, FIRST (For Inspiration and Recognition of Science and Technology) Robotics is the shining example of what a robotics competition should be. To this day, nearly every

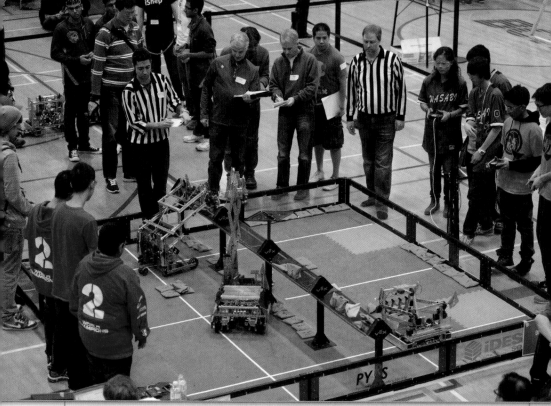

Teams compete in the 2013 VEX Robotics Competition, where robots are required to score by placing beanbag game pieces in raised goals.

successful competition for grade-school-aged students has been an attempt to replicate FIRST.

FIRST LEGO LEAGUE

As the name implies, FIRST Lego League (FLL) robots are based on Lego components. Participation is limited to students in fourth to eighth grade, ages nine to sixteen. The competition relies on the Mindstorms platform as the basis for FLL robots. In these competitions, teams run their robots autonomously to complete a series of missions outlined in the game description. Unique among the other competitions, FLL is about more than just robots. Every season, teams conduct a research project relevant to the year's game. Adding this component creates a well-rounded educational experience for all participants.

FIRST TECH CHALLENGE

Moving up the FIRST ranks, First Tech Challenge (FTC) is for middle and high school students in grades seven to twelve. Teams of up to ten students must build a robot that starts a match within an 18-inch (45.7 cm) cube. During a match, four robots, all from different teams, play in two-team alliances on a 12 ft × 12 ft (3.66 m × 3.66 m) field. In this competition, teams are permitted to use the Tetrix and Matrix robot platforms along with Lego pieces and the Lego Mindstorms control system. Each match consists of a thirty-second autonomous period followed by a two-minute driver-controlled period. If you have an experienced team with a limited budget, or if you're just getting started, FTC is the competition for you.

FIRST ROBOTICS COMPETITION

For those with a larger team, budget, or both and more technical experience, there is the FIRST Robotics Competition (FRC). FRC is designed for high school students, but it is open to students ages eighteen and under. A game is released the first weekend in January, and teams are given six weeks to design, build, program, and

ILITE Robotics

Located in Haymarket, Virginia, ILITE Robotics (Inspiring Leaders in Technology and Engineering) is an example of a FIRST Robotics team. FIRST is about more than just building robots; it's about advancing STEM education and improving the community at large. ILITE began as FRC team 1885 in 2006. Since then they have expanded, adding more and more FIRST teams, including ten FTC teams. In addition to actively running these teams, they also mentor external FTC and FLL teams. ILITE hosts three competitions a year: IROC (ILITE Robotics Offseason Challenge), the Northern Virginia FTC Qualifier, and the Haymarket FLL Regional. FIRST competitions are made possible because of the efforts made by the teams themselves. FRC teams around the country host competitions for other FIRST divisions. ILITE is one of many FIRST teams out there that have created successful programs for inspiring students to focus on STEM education. If you have the opportunity, you should absolutely look into joining a FIRST team.

test their robots. Robots designed for the FRC are unlike any other in the world.

Depending on the game rules, robots are allowed to expand once the match begins. Rules are not nearly as limited as they are in other competitions: robots can be built from almost any material, including metal, wood, and plastic. FIRST worked with NI to develop a universal control system for all FRC robots based off of NI's CompactRIO (cRIO) real-time embedded controller. As these robots are significantly more complicated, it is best to work with a large team of students and adult mentors.

BECOMING PART OF A TEAM

Teamwork is a major component of robotics. Everyone on the team has the same goal: to build an awesome, successful robot.

If any of these competitions sound interesting, it's time to look for a team. Most robotics competitions have a way to search for local teams. Many schools and youth organizations have already established teams. Take a look around and see if there is a team for you. If not, it might be time to start your own.

Each of these robotics competitions is incredibly exciting, but you can't make a team by yourself. If you want to start a team, you will need to find a group of other interested people around your age. It is also important to find a few mentors who have some experience to help guide you through the season. Your local makerspace is a great place to start recruiting, but there's no reason to stop there. Invite friends and classmates, and broadcast to your community that you're starting a team. Charitable organizations and companies in your area may be willing to help support your team, so you'll want to reach out to them as well.

Adult mentors are a key part of a successful robotics team. Try to recruit mentors with engineering and/or software experience to work with your team and help you develop your skills. Mentors are there to help guide you through any struggles you may run into along the way. The most successful robotics teams form a partnership with their community to keep mentors actively engaged. Remember, adults like to build robots, too.

If you've enjoyed working with robots, or if they just sound cool, working on a robotics team is something you should pursue.

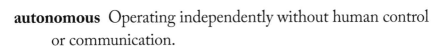

autonomous Operating independently without human control or communication.

breadboard An electronics prototyping tool used to quickly test a circuit.

circuit A group of individual electrical components connected together to perform an operation.

firmware The low-level software stored permanently in read-only memory that controls programs running on the device.

integrated circuit (IC) A circuit built into a single, small semiconductor chip.

integrated development environment (IDE) Software designed to ease the development process.

I/O port A connection used for input to and output from an external device.

makerspace A community center with shared tools and resources where people can work on projects.

manipulator A device, commonly attached to a robot chassis, used to control external objects.

microcontroller A small computer containing a processor, memory, and peripherals built onto a single IC.

open-source A model that provides a free license to a product or software design.

prototype An early model built to test a new product or feature design.

roboticist An individual who designs, builds, programs, and/or tests robots.

schematic A drawing of an electronic circuit design.

sensor A device used to detect and measure real-world characteristics.

software library A collection of code with a common interface for use in other software.

subsystem A system within a larger system.

syntax A set of rules that define software structure.

teleoperation Human operation of a robot from a distance.

traverse To move across a given area.

FIRST
200 Bedford Street
Manchester, NH 03101
(800) 871-8326
Website: http://www.usfirst.org
FIRST is the organization behind the largest grade school robotics in the United States. Its work has taken STEM education to a new level with hands-on engineering practices.

Let's Talk Science
1584 North Routledge Park
London, ON N6H 5L6
Canada
(877) 474-4081
Website: http://www.letstalkscience.ca
Let's Talk Science is a Canadian charitable organization devoted to inspiring and engaging students across Canada to get involved in STEM.

Make It @ Your Library
info@makeitatyourlibrary.org
Website: http://makeitatyourlibrary.org
This online resource provides ideas and instructions for projects that can be built at your local library makerspace.

Maker Media, Inc.
1005 Gravenstein Highway North
Sebastopol, CA 95472
Website: http://makermedia.com

Maker Media is the main driver behind the makerspace movement. It publishes *Make* magazine, operates Makezine.com, and hosts Maker Faires across the world.

Robotics Institute at Carnegie Mellon
5000 Forbes Avenue
Pittsburgh, PA 15213-3890
(412) 268-3818
Website: http://www.ri.cmu.edu
A global leader in robotics innovations, the Robotics Institute at Carnegie Mellon serves as a prime example of what a top educational institute can do.

US STEM Foundation
7371 Atlas Walk Way, #242
Gainesville, VA 20155
Website: http://www.usstem.org
The US STEM Foundation is a nonprofit organization with the goal of improving STEM education in the United States by connecting existing communities to create a broad support for STEM.

WEBSITES

Due to the changing nature of Internet links, Rosen Publishing has developed an online list of websites related to the subject of this book. This site is updated regularly. Please use this link to access the list:

http://www.rosenlinks.com/MAKER/Robot

Anderson, Chris. *Makers*. New York, NY: Crown Business, 2012.

Baichtal, John, Matthew Beckler, and Adam Wolf. *Make: Lego and Arduino Projects*. Sebastopol, CA: Maker Media, Inc, 2012.

Bascomb, Neal. *The New Cool*. New York, NY: Broadway Paperbacks, 2011.

Benedettelli, Daniele. *The Lego Mindstorms EV3 Laboratory*. San Francisco, CA: No Starch Press, 2013.

Cook, David. *Robot Building for Beginners*. New York, NY: Apress Media, 2010.

Cutcher, Dave. *Electronic Circuits for the Evil Genius*. New York, NY: McGraw-Hill, 2010.

Hatch, Mark. *The Maker Movement Manifesto*. New York, NY: McGraw-Hill, 2013.

Karvinen, Tero, and Kimmo Karvinen. *Make: Arduino Bots and Gadgets*. Sebastopol, CA: Maker Media, Inc., 2011.

Kemp, Adam. *The Makerspace Workbench*. Sebastopol, CA: Maker Media, Inc., 2013.

Kmieć, Paweł "Sariel." *The Unofficial Lego Technic Builder's Guide*. San Francisco, CA: No Starch Press, 2012.

Margolis, Michael. *Make an Arduino-Controlled Robot*. Sebastopol, CA: Maker Media, Inc., 2012.

McComb, Gordon. *Robot Builder's Bonanza*. New York, NY: McGraw-Hill, 2011.

Monk, Simon. *Programming Arduino*. New York, NY: McGraw-Hill, 2011.

Purdum, Jack. *Beginning C for Arduino*. New York, NY: Apress Media, 2012.

Trobaugh, James. *Winning Design! Lego Mindstorms NXT*. New York, NY: Apress Media, 2010.

FIRST. "FIRST Progression of Programs." 2013. Retrieved January 8, 2014 (http://www.usfirst.org/roboticsprograms).

Grinberg, Michael. "Building an Arduino Robot, Part I: Hardware Components." 2013. Retrieved November 27, 2013 (http://blog.miguelgrinberg.com).

Innovation First International. "VEX Robotics Design System." 2013. Retrieved December 26, 2013 (http://www.vexrobotics.com/vex).

Lego Group. "Lego Mindstorms EV3 Overview." 2013. Retrieved November 23, 2013 (http://education.lego.com).

Lego Group. *NXT User Guide*. Billund Municipality, Denmark: The Lego Group, 2006.

Matrix Robotics International. "Matrix Robotics Products." 2013. Retrieved December 26, 2013 (http://matrixrobotics.com).

MIT Sea Grant. "Sea Perch Construction Manual." 2008. Retrieved December 16, 2013 (https://seaperch.mit.edu).

PITSCO Education. "Tetrix Building System." 2013. Retrieved December 26, 2013 (http://tetrixrobotics.org).

Robotics Education and Competition Foundation. "VEX Robotics Competition Overview." 2013. Retrieved January 8, 2014 (http://www.roboticseducation.org).

Schaefer, Carl. *ECE 450: Introduction to Robotics Lecture Notes*. Fairfax, VA: George Mason University ECE Department, 2013.

SparkFun Electronics. "Beatty Robotics Builds Mars Rover, Blows Our Minds." June 19, 2013. Retrieved January 5, 2014 (https://www.sparkfun.com/news/1159).

ABOUT THE AUTHOR

Jacob Cohen is a graduate of George Mason University with a BS in computer engineering specializing in robotics and embedded systems. As a FIRST Robotics alumnus and mentor of ILITE Robotics, Cohen has seen firsthand the benefits of robotics education. He has coached elementary, middle, and high school robotics teams in the classroom and on the playing field. For the last four years, he has served as an FLL Robot Design judge, and he was named FLL Regional Volunteer of the Year. Cohen is a constant advocate for STEM education, serving on the board of directors for the US STEM Foundation.

PHOTO CREDITS

Cover, p. 1 Kurita Kaku/Gamma-Rapho/Getty Images; pp. 4-5, 14, 24 (bottom), 32, 37 © AP Images; pp. 7, 15, 19, 25, 31, 36, 41, 48 © iStockphoto. com/Mordolff; p. 8 Larry Burrows/Time & Life Pictures/Getty Images; p. 10 © Imago/ZUMA Press; p. 11 U.S. Marine Corps photo by Lance Cpl. M. L. Meier/Wikimedia Commons/File: Big dog military robots.jpg; p. 16 edography/Shutterstock.com; pp. 18, 24 (top), 33 Chelle Hambric, ILITE Robotics; p. 20 Johan Swanepoel/Shutterstock.com; p. 26 Junko Kimura/Getty Images; p. 30 LEGO/AP Images; p. 39 Courtesy of VEX Robotics, Inc.; p. 42 © iStockphoto.com/luxxtek; p. 44 Dhesley1519/Wikimedia Commons/File: Arduino motor shield 11-4-13.jpg/CC BY-SA 3.0; p. 47 Marcmccomb/Wikimedia Commons/File: Line follower.jpg/ CC BY-SA 3.0; p. 49 Gabriela Hasbun/Redux; p. 52 © Sergei Bachlakov/Xinhua/ZUMA Press; cover and interior page design elements © iStockphoto.com/Samarskaya (cover wires), © iStockphoto.com/klenger (interior wires), © iStockphoto.com/A-Digit (circuit board design), © iStockphoto.com/Steven van Soldt (metal plate), © iStockphoto.com/Storman (background pp. 4–5).

Designer: Nelson Sá; Editor: Nicholas Croce;
Photo Researcher: Karen Huang